13 Colonies

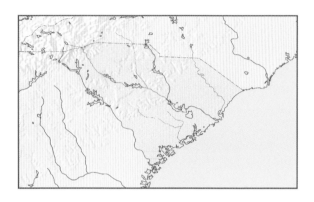

SOUTH CAROLINA

13 Colonies

SOUTH CAROLINA

THE HISTORY OF SOUTH CAROLINA COLONY, 1670–1776

ROBERTA WIENER AND JAMES R. ARNOLD

Raintree

Chicago, Illinois

Printed in China by South China Printing.
09 08 07 06 05
10 9 8 7 6 5 4 3 2 1

Library of Congress Cataloging-in-Publication Data
Wiener, Roberta, 1952-
  South Carolina / Roberta Wiener and James R. Arnold.
    p. cm. -- (13 colonies)
Includes bibliographical references (p.) and index.
Contents: The English come to Charles Town -- South Carolina in 1670 -- Charles Town and the low country: the early years -- South Carolina in war and peace -- The growing colony -- A world at war -- The road to revolution -- Glossary.
  ISBN 0-7398-6888-8 (lib. bdg.) -- ISBN 1-4109-0312-5 (pbk.)
  1. South Carolina--History--Colonial period, ca. 1600-1775--Juvenile literature. 2. South Carolina--History--Revolution, 1775-1783--Juvenile literature. [1. South Carolina--History--Colonial period, ca. 1600-1775. 2. South Carolina--History--Revolution, 1775-1783.] I. Arnold, James R. II. Title. II. Series: Wiener, Roberta, 1952- 13 colonies.
  F272.W63 2004
  975.7'02--dc22
                    2003021097

Every effort has been made to contact copyright holders of any material reproduced in this book. Any omissions will be rectified in subsequent printings if notice is given to the publishers.

Disclaimer
All the Internet addresses (URLs) given in this book were valid at the time of going to press. However, due to the dynamic nature of the Internet, some addresses may have changed, or sites may have changed or ceased to exist since publication. While the author and publishers regret any inconvenience this may cause readers, no responsibility for any such changes can be accepted by either the author or the publishers.

The paper used to print this book comes from sustainable resources.

Some words are shown in bold, **like this.** You can find out what they mean by looking in the glossary.

Title page picture: Rows of slave cabins at Mulberry House, a fine South Carolina plantation house.

Opposite: Charles Town in 1760.

The authors wish to thank Walter Kossmann, whose knowledge, patience, and ability to ask all the right questions have made this a better series.

PICTURE ACKNOWLEDGMENTS

ARCHITECT OF THE CAPITOL: 7 ARIZONA HISTORICAL SOCIETY: 46-47 AUTHORS: 37 WILLIAM CULLEN BRYANT, ET. AL., *Scribner's Popular History of the United States*, 1896: 14, 21, 29 bottom COLONIAL WILLIAMSBURG FOUNDATION: Cover, 5, 6, 12, 30-31, 33 GIBBES MUSEUM OF ART/CAROLINA ART ASSOCIATION: Title page, 29 top, 38-39, 40 COURTESY OF HARGRETT RARE BOOK & MANUSCRIPT LIBRARY/UNIVERSITY OF GEORGIA LIBRARIES: 48-49 COURTESY OF THE HISTORICAL SOCIETY OF DELAWARE: 44 top *Howard Pyle's Book of the American Spirit*, 1923: 43 INDEPENDENCE NATIONAL HISTORICAL PARK: 52, 53 top LIBRARY OF CONGRESS: 18 top, 20, 22-23, 25, 28, 36, 53 bottom BENSON J. LOSSING, *Our Country: A Household History of the United States*, 1895: 16, 47 NATIONAL ARCHIVES: 8, 44 bottom I. N. PHELPS STOKES COLLECTION, NEW YORK PUBLIC LIBRARY: 51 COURTESY OF THE NORTH CAROLINA OFFICE OF ARCHIVES AND HISTORY: 9, 10, 13, 19, 34, 41, 45 U.S. SENATE COLLECTION: 54, 55 SOUTH CAROLINA HISTORICAL SOCIETY: 15, 27, 50, 59 COURTESY OF SOUTH CAROLINIANA LIBRARY, UNIVERSITY OF SOUTH CAROLINA, COLUMBIA: 32, 35, 42 TENNESSEE STATE MUSEUM: 56-57

CONTENTS

PROLOGUE: THE WORLD IN 1670   6
1. THE ENGLISH COME TO CHARLES TOWN   12
2. SOUTH CAROLINA IN 1670   17
3. CHARLES TOWN AND THE LOW COUNTRY:
   THE EARLY YEARS   21
4. SOUTH CAROLINA IN WAR AND PEACE   25
5. THE GROWING COLONY   29
6. A WORLD AT WAR   45
7. THE ROAD TO REVOLUTION   51
EPILOGUE   58
DATELINE   60
GLOSSARY   61
FURTHER READING   62
WEBSITES   63
BIBLIOGRAPHY   63
INDEX   64

PROLOGUE: THE WORLD IN 1670

By the year 1670, Europeans had been exploring the world for close to 200 years. Advances in navigation and the building of better sailing ships made longer voyages possible. Great navigators from Portugal, Spain, Italy, the Netherlands, France, and England sailed into uncharted waters. The explorers reached Africa, India, the Pacific Ocean, China, Japan, and Australia. They encountered kingdoms and civilizations that had existed for centuries.

Europeans did not yet have a clear idea where all these lands lay, but they knew enough to see great opportunity. They saw the chance to grow rich from trade in exotic spices. They saw souls they wanted to convert to Christianity. They saw the chance to make conquests and expand their countries into great empires. And not least, they encountered the dark-skinned people of Africa and, thinking them a different species, saw the chance to capture and sell slaves.

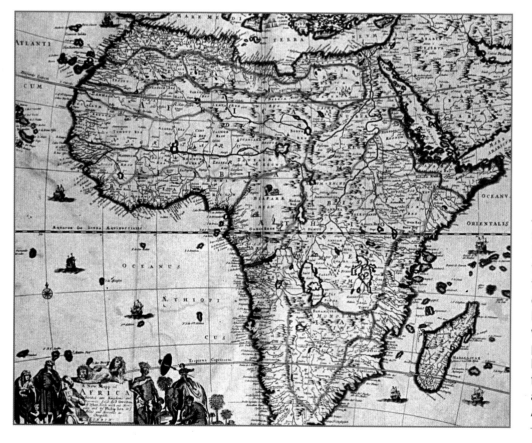

Slaves captured in Africa were forced to march to the west coast of the continent. From there, they were tightly packed into European ships for the voyage across the Atlantic Ocean.

All the voyagers from Europe to the lands of the Pacific Ocean had to sail around Africa, a long and dangerous journey. So European explorers began to sail westward in search of a shorter route. In 1492, the explorer Christopher Columbus landed on an island on the far side of the Atlantic Ocean and claimed it for Spain. He thought that he had actually sailed all the way around the world and come to an island near India. Years of exploration by numerous sailors passed before the people of Europe realized that Columbus had been the first European of their era to set foot in a land unknown to them. They called this land the New World, although it was not new to the people who lived there.

A succession of explorers and would-be colonists from Spain, France, and England walked on the soil of the Carolinas during the 1500s. Several tried to establish permanent settlements. All of them failed.

Many artists have imagined and made pictures of Columbus coming ashore on the far side of the Atlantic.

DOMESTIC: TAME, REFERRING TO ANIMALS SUCH AS LIVESTOCK

WEST INDIES: ISLANDS OF THE CARIBBEAN SEA, SO CALLED BECAUSE THE FIRST EUROPEAN VISITORS THOUGHT THEY WERE NEAR INDIA

MALARIA: POTENTIALLY FATAL DISEASE SPREAD BY MOSQUITOS

The Spanish brought the first domestic horses to America in 1539, and the first domestic cattle in 1550. Some of these animals were lost or abandoned and lived in the wild.

The Spanish quickly surpassed England and France in the competition for land in the Americas. Before either the English or the French had settled in America, the Spanish had already claimed huge portions of both North and South America for Spain and established bases in the islands of the **West Indies**. In 1521, a Spanish sea captain captured about 100 Native Americans on the coast of South Carolina and brought them to the West Indies as slaves. Most of the captives died, but one lived long enough to convince the Spanish that his country was full of gold. Lured by the reports of gold, in 1526, about 500 Spanish men and women, led by Lucas Vásquez de Ayllón, set out from a Caribbean island and settled on the South Carolina coast. Many died of **malaria** or hunger. Finally, about 150 survivors abandoned the settlement and returned to the Caribbean.

Undaunted by failure, the Spanish went on to conquer the Inca empire in South America. They brought the first **domestic** horses to the Americas, and established a printing press and a university. They explored much of South and Central America, and the southern part of North America. The Spanish explorer Hernando de Soto led a party of soldiers overland from Florida, crossing the western part of the Carolinas in 1540. He was searching for gold, and he found the Mississippi River.

France also sent explorers to North America. In 1524, the Italian Giovanni da Verrazano, working for France, sailed along the coast from North Carolina to New England. Far to the north, Jacques Cartier began exploring part of eastern Canada in 1534, but he failed to establish a colony. Based on these voyages, in 1562 France risked the anger of Spain and planned an American colony as a refuge for French Protestants.

Concerned that their future in predominantly **Catholic** France looked bleak, an expedition of French Protestants, called Huguenots, sailed for America under the leadership of Jean Ribault. Ribault left about 30 men near present-day Port Royal, South Carolina, where they built a fort called Charlesfort. Ribault returned to France for more supplies and colonists. By the time he arrived in France, the Catholics and Protestants were fighting one another. The resulting bloody Wars of Religion were to last for more than 35 years.

The start of war in France prevented Ribault from returning to aid his colony. The men left behind at Charlesfort ran out of food. Rebelling and killing their commander, they built a ship and sailed for France. Two years later, in 1564, another party of French Huguenots tried to establish an American colony. They built Fort Caroline on the coast of Florida. In 1565 the Spanish founded St. Augustine, Florida

CATHOLIC: ROMAN CATHOLIC; THE OLDEST CHRISTIAN CHURCH ORGANIZATION, GOVERNED BY A HIERARCHY BASED IN ROME

Ribault's men succeeded in building a ship and setting sail, but they ran out of food during the voyage. Finally, the starving men were rescued at sea by a British ship, but not before they had resorted to cannibalism. The survivors became prisoners of the British, but some eventually returned to France.

settlement, the first permanent settlement in what would become the United States. From there, the Spanish quickly attacked Fort Caroline and killed its occupants.

The Spanish built a string of forts in the region to keep other Europeans away. One of these, San Felipe, was on present-day Parris Island, South Carolina. A mission and farms grew up around the fort. However, the Spanish in South Carolina endured food shortages and attacks by Native Americans. Finally, in 1587, the English admiral Sir Francis Drake burned St. Augustine. Drake's attack caused the Spanish to withdraw from South Carolina to concentrate on defending their remaining possessions.

England and Spain had long been enemies, but they did not officially declare war until 1587. In the meantime, the Englishman Walter Raleigh had sponsored several voyages to explore the American coast and to establish an English colony. The first voyagers, in 1584, explored the coast of the Carolinas and claimed a vast area for England. They didn't stay, however. Raleigh called the new land Virginia, in honor of Queen Elizabeth I, who was known as the Virgin Queen because she never married.

Raleigh then sent a new expedition to Virginia in 1585. He planned for the settlers to establish an English military outpost from which they could attack Spanish ships. The expedition landed in what is now North Carolina. The first group gave up and returned to England in 1586. A second group, sent in 1587, disappeared

The Spanish fort on Parris Island. The English Admiral Sir Francis Drake had been sailing the seas of the world for nearly ten years before his attack on St. Augustine convinced the Spanish to withdraw from South Carolina.

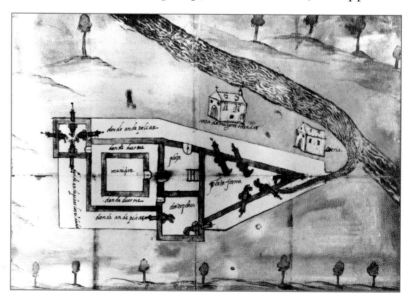

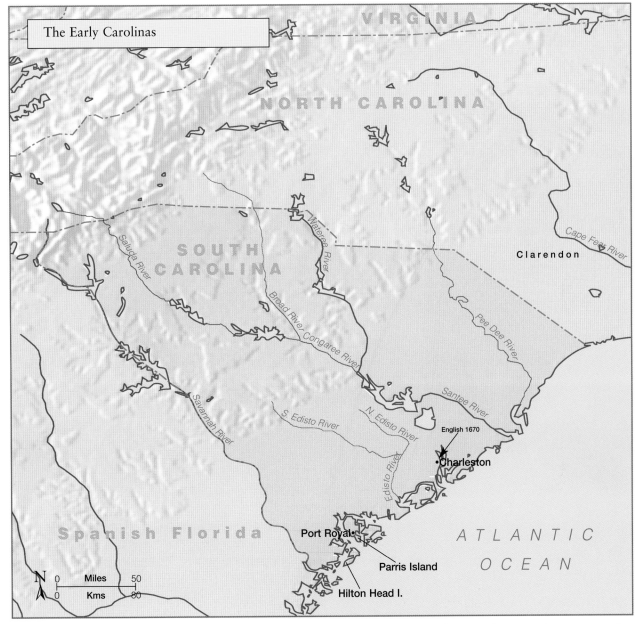

The Early Carolinas

without a trace, and their settlement became known as the Lost Colony. [The story of the Lost Colony is told in the book about North Carolina.]

Although England laid claim to the Carolinas, many years passed before English people again tried to live there. By that time, English settlements stretched from present-day Maine to the Virginia–North Carolina border. By 1670, these settlements were home to more than 100,000 English colonists.

I.
THE ENGLISH COME TO CHARLES TOWN

In 1629, King Charles I granted a **charter** to one of his officials, Sir Robert Heath. The king gave the name "Carolana" to an area extending from Spanish Florida to Virginia. Heath made plans to colonize the land but had no success. Heath gave up his charter and other men tried to start a new colony, publishing pamphlets in an effort to stimulate interest among the English.

The first English people to live in the land of Carolana were settled from Jamestown. In fact, they saw Carolana as simply the southern part of Virginia. By the 1650s, Virginians were going south to buy land from the Native Americans, and the Virginia government was making land grants in the region. As Virginia's population grew and land became scarce, more traders and farmers bought land from the Native Americans and expanded southward into the area around the Albemarle Sound. In 1662, Virginia's governor appointed officials to govern what he called the "Southern **Plantation**."

England was plunged into civil war in 1642, and King Charles I was executed by his enemies in 1649. After nearly 10 years in exile, the son of Charles I won back the throne and became King Charles II in 1660. The new king rewarded eight of his most loyal supporters by granting them the vast area of Carolana, renaming it Carolina. The land grant extended not only from Florida to Virginia, but all the way to the Pacific Ocean. The **proprietors** divided Carolina into the provinces of Albemarle, the northeastern part of North Carolina bordering Virginia, and Clarendon, from the Cape Fear River southward toward present-day South Carolina.

The charter of March 24, 1663, gave the new proprietors power to grant land, appoint public officials, collect taxes, and raise armies to conduct wars. The proprietors also agreed to tolerate religions that differed from the Church of England. They did so out of a desire to attract settlers and increase the English population, rather than from a firm belief in religious freedom.

King Charles I ruled England from 1625 to 1649.

CHARTER: DOCUMENT CONTAINING THE RULES FOR RUNNING AN ORGANIZATION

PLANTATION: LARGE ESTATE WHERE A CASH CROP IS GROWN, USUALLY FARMED BY SLAVES

One of the proprietors, Sir William Berkeley, was already the governor of Virginia. Two others, Lord John Berkeley, William's brother, and Sir George Carteret were also the proprietors of the New Jersey colony. The other five proprietors were George Monck, the Duke of Albemarle; Edward Hyde, Earl of Clarendon; Lord William Craven; Anthony Ashley Cooper, Earl of Shaftesbury; and Sir John Colleton, a **planter** on the island of Barbados, an English colony in the West Indies. Most of these proprietors were content to rule their colony from a distance.

Virginia settlers who arrived before Carolina was chartered lived a pioneer's life of **subsistence** farming and handmade goods. They cut down the trees to clear land,

PLANTER: OWNER OF A LARGE ESTATE, CALLED A PLANTATION

SUBSISTENCE: PRODUCING JUST ENOUGH FOOD OR INCOME TO SURVIVE

Carolina's Charter of 1663 granted a vast territory to be shared by eight proprietors.

Captain Hilton's party approaches the land that came to be called Hilton Head, on the coast of South Carolina.

build log cabins, and fuel their cooking fires. The new proprietors, however, expected to make money by granting large tracts of land and collecting rents. They were not looking for pioneers who wanted to make a bare living on small farms. The proprietors tried to recruit settlers from New England and Barbados. A group of New Englanders began a settlement on the Cape Fear River, but they did not like the area and returned home.

Captain William Hilton led an expedition from Barbados to explore the Carolina coast southward from the Cape Fear region in August 1663. After a voyage of about two weeks the party reached Carolina and sailed into the harbor of Port Royal, where they rescued several shipwrecked Englishmen who were living among the Native Americans. On their return to Barbados, the explorers published a report of their voyage that did much to raise interest in settlement. Hilton Head Island is named after Captain Hilton. In 1666, the proprietors invited English colonists from Barbados to build a settlement on the Cape Fear River. Within two years they had abandoned the settlement.

In 1669, the proprietors put into effect the "Fundamental Constitutions of Carolina." This document called for a **feudal** society based on members of the **nobility** owning large tracts of land that would be worked by tenant farmers or slaves. However, it continued the elected legislature and the policy of religious tolerance for non-**Anglican** Christians, stating "No person whatsoever shall disturb, molest, or persecute another, for his speculative opinions in religion, or his way of worship." The 1669 constitution gave Jews as well the right to practice their religion in Carolina. The proprietors may have been trying to attract the many prosperous Jewish traders who lived on Barbados in order to expand Carolina's white population. Many Jews eventually chose to live in Charles Town, where they prospered in business. The proprietors also encouraged people to settle in Carolina by offering generous grants of land.

By 1670, the small island of Barbados was extremely crowded, with more than 30,000 people on an island of 166 square miles. A few wealthy English planters owned huge sugar plantations, leaving little land for the growing population. Only the very wealthy were able to make a good profit growing sugarcane. Therefore, many islanders were attracted by the chance to acquire land in Carolina and leave great plantations to their children. The proprietors granted colonists from 50 to 150 acres of Carolina land per family member or slave, and set a rent of less than a penny per acre, with no payment due until 1689. Planters wealthy enough to own numerous slaves

FEUDAL: SYSTEM IN MEDIEVAL EUROPE UNDER WHICH LANDLESS FARMERS LIVED AND WORKED ON LAND OWNED BY OTHERS

NOBILITY: MEMBERS OF THE HIGH BRITISH SOCIAL CLASS JUST BELOW ROYALTY, POSSESSING TITLES OR RANKS THAT WERE EITHER INHERITED OR GIVEN BY THE KING OR QUEEN

ANGLICAN: BELONGING TO THE CHURCH OF ENGLAND, A PROTESTANT CHURCH AND THE STATE CHURCH OF ENGLAND

A map of Carolina made in 1666, not long after Hilton's voyage.

received huge tracts of land. However, they came to resent paying even a penny per acre and used a variety of tricks to avoid paying.

The proprietors paid for three ships to take about 150 people from England to Port Royal on the Carolina coast. The ships sailed from England in August 1669, and first stopped at Barbados to pick up more colonists. After enduring an extraordinary series of storms and shipwrecks, the colonists arrived at Carolina in April 1670.

The newly arrived colonists settled on the Ashley River at Albemarle Point. A few months later, they named their settlement Charles Town (Charleston in present-day South Carolina), after King Charles II of England. Settlers continued to arrive from Barbados, bringing slaves along. After two years, the area around Charles Town had an estimated population of about 250 English people and 100 African slaves. At first, men outnumbered women two to one, as was typical in new settlements in the colonies.

From the new settlement of Charles Town, English colonists spread out to establish large plantations in the surrounding countryside. Some planters avoided making rent payments on the land by not registering their land, or just by not paying.

2.
SOUTH CAROLINA IN 1670

The Coastal Plain, also called the Low Country, is a land of sandy soil and swamps. The land of the low country rises gradually from the sea islands along the coast, westward to the pine tree–covered sand hills. Next comes the **Piedmont**, hilly and forested. The Blue Ridge Mountains occupy the far northwestern corner of the state. The highest point is Sassafras Mountain at 3,560 feet (1,085 meters). The Piedmont and mountains together are commonly called the Up Country. From west to east flow the Saluda, Broad, Wateree, Congaree, Pee Dee, Santee, Edisto, and Savannah Rivers. The Savannah River forms the border between South Carolina and Georgia.

> **PIEDMONT: HILLY REGION BETWEEN THE LOW COUNTRY AND THE MOUNTAINS**

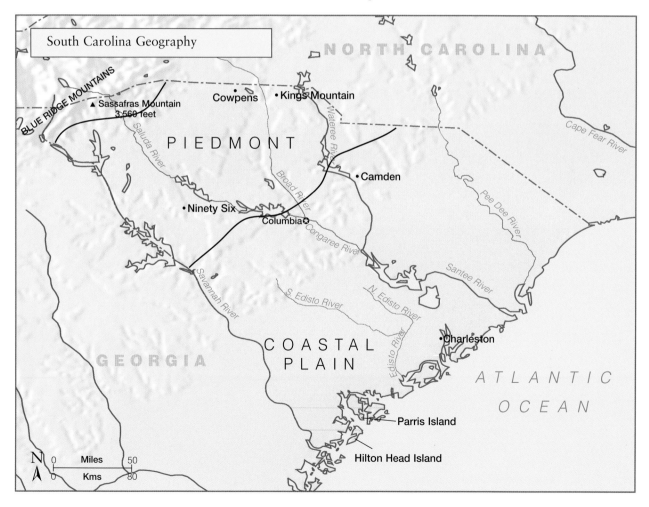

South Carolina Geography

Native Americans known as "mound builders" lived in the Carolinas until about 900 years ago. They built huge dirt mounds—probably for a combination of defense, religious ceremonies, and burials —by hauling baskets full of dirt on their backs. Like later Native Americans, they also grew corn.

South Carolina has a warm climate with plentiful rain. Winter temperatures usually stay above freezing and snow is rare, except in the mountains. The state sometimes suffers severe damage from hurricanes. The southeastern part of the coastal plain is subtropical, with alligators and palmetto trees, as well as Venus flytraps. Large flocks of ducks and geese spend winters along the coast and in the swamps.

Numerous Native American tribes inhabited the land that became South Carolina. The first may have arrived there 12,000 years ago. During the 1600s, an estimated 20,000 Native Americans lived in South Carolina. Contact with European colonists quickly reduced the Native American population. They suffered and died from diseases such as smallpox, which they caught from Europeans. The Native American tribes also fought one another for territory and, later, for the chance to trade with the English.

Along the coast lived the Cusabo, Sewee, Westo, and Yamassee Indians. The Wateree, Santee, Congaree, and Catawba lived farther inland, in the marshes and along the rivers of the Piedmont. Still farther west lived the Cherokee, in the mountains of South Carolina, North Carolina, Georgia, and Tennessee. They

The Englishman John Lawson observed the wildlife of Carolina, including alligators: "This amphibious monster dwells all winter, sleeping away his time till the Spring appears. ... He never devours men in Carolina, but uses all ways to avoid them, yet he kills swine and dogs ... ."

often fought the Catawba for land and tried to expand into their territory.

The Native Americans lived in villages surrounded by protective fences. They built their houses of bark and woven mats placed over a framework of poles. Near their homes they prepared large fields for farming. They made small mounds within these fields where they planted corn along with squash and beans. They also grew tobacco, and eventually introduced the English to smoking. During the summer, women tended the fields, which the men had cleared. They usually managed to grow or find just enough

While exploring the Carolina coast in 1584, English people met Native Americans, and the English artist John White painted pictures of them and their villages. The Native Americans welcomed the opportunity to trade with the explorers, especially for goods that might give them an advantage over their enemies. Wrote the English captain of a Native American, "When we showed him all our packet of merchandise, of all the things that he saw, a bright tin dish most pleased him, which he presently took up and clapped it before his breast, and after made a hole in the brim thereof and hung it about his neck, making signs that it would defend him against his enemies' arrows … ."

Bison, also called buffalo, lived in the Carolinas as late as 1709, according to English settler John Lawson. He wrote, "The buffalo is a wild beast of America … his chief haunt being the land of the Mississippi … yet I have known some killed on the hilly part of Cape Fear River."

food to survive. William Hilton reported that "the Indians plant in the worst land, because they cannot cut down the timber in the best, and yet have plenty of corn …".

The Native Americans also lived by hunting and fishing. Carolina was rich in wildlife. The ocean and rivers yielded tremendous numbers of fish and shellfish. Huge flocks of waterfowl such as ducks and geese lived in the coastal marshes. The inland forests gave food and shelter to large populations of wild animals. Deer and deerskins provided food, clothing, and shelter.

The first European settlers hunted, too, killing bison, elk, cougars, and wolves until most disappeared from the area. European settlers introduced red foxes and wild pigs. Deer were plentiful, but the colonists' demand for deerskins encouraged the Native Americans to kill too many, and they severely reduced the deer population.

The land was heavily forested with pines, cypress, and hardwoods such as oak and hickory. William Hilton reported in 1664, "The lands are laden with large tall oaks, walnut and bayes, except facing on the sea, it is mostly pines tall and good. The land generally, except where the pines grow, is a good soil …. The country abounds with grapes, large figs, and peaches, the woods with deer … the rivers stored plentifully with fish that we saw play and leap …" When English colonists arrived, they cleared large areas of forest and planted crops.

3.
CHARLES TOWN AND THE LOW COUNTRY: THE EARLY YEARS

The first English settlers of Charles Town met the Cusabo Native Americans, who were eager to trade with them. The Cusabos also hoped the English would protect them from the Native Americans known as the Westos, who were invading their territory. The so-called Westos had once been part of the Erie people, but they had been driven from the shores of Lake Erie by the Iroquois of Pennsylvania and New York. They fled southward and eventually settled along the Savannah River during the 1650s. From their new base, the Westos kidnapped Cusabos and sold them as slaves to the English of Virginia.

The Spanish first enslaved some of Carolina's native peoples in 1521. More than 200 years later, the English were still doing so. Slave traders took captive Native Americans to the West Indies and exchanged two Native American slaves for one African slave. The African slaves were valued more highly because they were believed to survive longer and work harder than the Native Americans.

The early settlers planted tobacco, cotton and sugarcane, but they made most of their money by trading with the Native Americans, offering them metal tools, guns, and rum in exchange for deer and other animal skins. The colonists soon began trading with the more powerful Westos instead of the Cusabos. The Westos also captured women and children from enemy tribes and sold them to the English. In this way they soon destroyed the Cusabos. The trader Henry Woodward, reporting on his dealings with the Westo Indians, wrote in December 1674 that he expected to see them again in March 1675 "with deer skins, furs, and young slaves."

English traders expected the Native Americans to help them obtain and keep slaves. The Native Americans learned that if they helped runaway slaves, the English would attack them. If instead they captured and returned runaways, the English of Carolina rewarded them with a gun and three blankets per slave.

Around 1680, a competing group of English traders began doing business with a band of Shawnee Indians who had settled on the Savannah River, and were therefore called the Savannahs. The Savannahs began capturing the Westos and selling them to the English as slaves. Just as the Westos had destroyed the Cusabos, so the Savannahs destroyed the Westos. Before long it would be the Savannahs' turn to suffer the same fate at the hands of a stronger tribe.

The English forced some Native Americans to labor on their plantations, but many escaped by slipping into the familiar woods. About 1,500 Native American slaves labored on South Carolina plantations during the colony's first 50 years, but thousands more were shipped from Charles Town to the West Indies. The ships brought back African slaves on the return voyage. English sugar planters on Barbados treated their slaves with extreme cruelty. About 250,000 African slaves were brought to the West Indies during the 1600s, but only about one in three survived more than a couple of years. They succumbed to being overworked in extreme heat, brutally beaten, and poorly fed. The colonists who came from Barbados to Charles Town continued to treat their slaves with the same inhumanity. The Carolina constitution of 1669 had granted "every **freeman** of Carolina … absolute power and authority over his negro slaves."

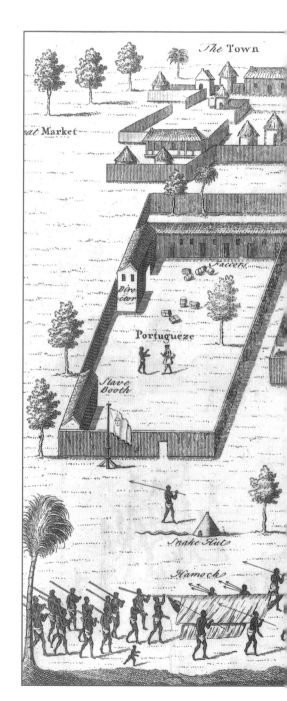

A camp on the west coast of Africa, where European traders purchased African slaves from their captors.

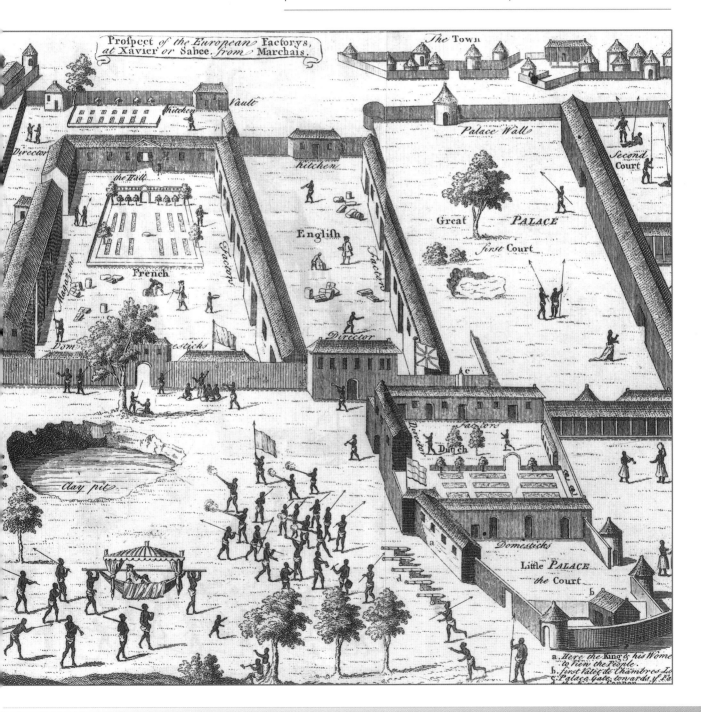

MERCHANT: TRADER;
PERSON WHO BUYS AND
RESELLS MERCHANDISE

South Carolina's climate made it a good place to raise livestock. The colony became a leading cattle producer. Cattle were herded across the Carolinas to Charles Town to be sold and slaughtered. Meat had to be salted, smoked, or dried before it could be exported. The South Carolina town of Cowpens was named for its role as a way station on the cattle drives. Livestock remains an important part of South Carolina agriculture.

Charles Town **merchants** sent most of their trade goods to ports in the West Indies, which were much closer than ports in England. The merchants continued to export animal skins and furs that traders purchased from the Native Americans. South Carolina exported more than 50,000 deerskins per year during the early 1700s. Farmers and planters raised cattle and hogs, which could live out of doors all winter long in South Carolina's warm climate and find plenty to eat in the wild. Livestock became another important early export, as did corn.

The Low Country planters of Carolina began growing rice in swampy areas during the 1680s after a ship captain brought some seeds from Madagascar. Their slaves planted the rice in the springtime, and the fields were flooded in the summer. Slaves harvested the rice in early autumn and separated the grains of rice from the stalks, and then spent long hours pounding the grains of rice to remove the husks. Some slaves had grown rice in Africa, so they knew more than their masters about how to care for the crop and extract the final product. Over time, rice grew in economic importance.

During the 1740s, indigo became another important money-making crop for South Carolina planters. Lumber, as well as the naval stores of tar, pitch, and turpentine, all produced in the Low Country pinelands, also became major exports.

4.
SOUTH CAROLINA IN WAR AND PEACE

The English settlers of South Carolina had enemies on every side. The planters worried that they could be attacked on their own plantations by their slaves at any time. Traders believed that the Native Americans could turn against them without warning. Planters and traders alike feared that the French in the Mississippi Valley might attack from the west, or that the Spanish might attack from the south. The Spanish, French, and English all wanted to possess the land and control access to their Native American trading partners.

Most alarmingly, in 1702, France and Spain formed an alliance and went to war against England. In Charles Town, Governor James Moore decided the time was right to strike at the Spanish in St. Augustine before they

Charles Town was twice as close to Spanish St. Augustine (left) as it was to English Jamestown.

attacked the English. Charles Town and St. Augustine were only about 250 miles apart, a ten-day walk or a few days' sailing. However, only about 1,500 Spanish lived at St. Augustine, while more than twice as many English lived around Charles Town, so the English outnumbered the Spanish two to one.

Confident of success, Governor Moore sent eight ships to attack Spanish Florida. About 50 Carolinians and more than 1,000 Native Americans, including Creeks, Yamassees, and Savannahs, failed to breach the walls of St. Augustine. The Spanish, in turn, tried to attack Charles Town but they also failed. Over the next few years, Governor Moore's army ventured south through Georgia into northern Florida to raid communities of Native Americans who were loyal to the Spanish. The army burned Native American villages and captured thousands of Native Americans to be sold into slavery, destroying about three quarters of the Native American population in Spanish territory.

THE YAMASSEE WAR

The Native American tribes of Carolina competed with one another for English trade goods, especially guns and ammunition. They hunted deer and captured people from rival tribes so they could buy firearms with which to defeat one another. They paid for their weapons with deerskins and human beings. The English traders set the prices high, demanding more and more deerskins and slaves. In trying to meet the English traders' growing demand for deerskins, the Native Americans killed too many deer, and deer became scarce. It became harder and harder for them to

Native American men hunted deer with guns they obtained from the English traders, and the women treated the deerskins to preserve them and make them flexible.

find deer to kill to pay for trade goods, so they fell into permanent debt to the white traders.

The traders ventured hundreds of miles westward and began trading with the Catawbas. In 1707, the Savannahs recognized that they would never be able to kill enough deer or capture enough slaves to pay the English traders what they demanded. The Savannahs tried to flee their overwhelming debt and go north to their Shawnee relatives in Pennsylvania, but the traders convinced the Catawbas to pursue the Savannahs and capture them as slaves. Very few escaped, and the Savannahs went the way of the Cusabos and Westos.

In 1711, the Tuscarora of North Carolina erupted into violence against the demanding traders and the increasing number of European settlers moving into their territory. In a coordinated surprise attack against colonial settlements, the Tuscarora killed about 130 settlers. During the next two years, hundreds of Yamassee warriors, led by South Carolina **militia** officers, marched north to help North Carolina defeat the Tuscarora. Cherokee, Creek, and Catawba also joined the South Carolina force. One of the leading officers was James Moore Jr., son of the former governor.

> MILITIA: GROUP OF CITIZENS NOT NORMALLY PART OF THE ARMY WHO JOIN TOGETHER TO DEFEND THEIR LAND IN AN EMERGENCY

Colonel John Barnwell of South Carolina led a war party to North Carolina to help the English fight the Tuscarora.

After helping the Carolinians finish off the Tuscarora, the Yamassee continued to trade with the English, and in time came to owe the traders more than 100,000 deerskins, an impossible number. In spite of the help the colonists had received from the Yamassees against the Tuscarora, traders began capturing Yamassee women and children to sell as slaves, as a way of collecting their debt. At the same time, the colonists turned to trading with the Cherokees and other tribes.

Furious at the enslavement of their people, in April 1715 the Yamassees, joined by the Creeks and Catawbas, attacked plantations around Port Royal. The Native Americans burned houses, slaughtered cattle, and killed traders and other colonists. Over several months, the united Native Americans killed more than 400 settlers. Many settlers fled to Charles Town, and the fighting ranged very close to the town walls. They became desperate enough to arm some slaves. Only the agreement of the Cherokees—long time enemies of the Yamassees—to fight on the side of the settlers turned the tide. In addition, surviving Tuscaroras returned to Carolina to take revenge on the Native Americans who had fought against them. Most of the Yamassee were killed or captured and sold into slavery. The rest fled from the colony and moved to the south. The Creeks retreated to the west, and the Catawbas signed a peace treaty with South Carolina.

The Yamassee' fierce attack on South Carolina plantations was intended to drive the English colonists out of the colony.

5.
THE GROWING COLONY

The end of the Tuscarora and Yamassee wars opened the way for more colonists to settle in the Carolinas. Native Americans withdrew to the west or were confined to reservations, their numbers reduced by war and disease. Where once thousands of Native Americans had lived, only a few hundred remained. Trade with the Native Americans diminished in importance as a way of making money in South Carolina, and agriculture expanded to take its place. The tide of white settlement swept across the colony. Huge plantations occupied the best land along the banks of the rivers. Good land for smaller farms was plentiful "up country" in the Piedmont region. Charles Town grew as the center of business, political, and social activity for the colony. It became the most important town

Above: During a five-year period, pirates took nearly 40 ships in the waters off Carolina. Shippers using the port of Charles Town were losing too many ships loaded with merchandise to pirates. Under orders from the governor of South Carolina, Colonel William Rhett (above) captured the legendary pirate, Stede Bonnet, in 1718.

Left: Many Carolina colonists were sympathetic to piracy. Some officials took bribes from pirates and turned a blind eye to their activities. Even the governors of the Carolinas welcomed pirates because they attacked enemy ships and helped guard the coast. Charles Town was a busy port, and hundreds of sailors, including pirates, spent time in its taverns.

in the south and served as the seaport for the neighboring colonies. Other southern colonies sent trade goods to Charles Town, from where they were shipped to foreign markets. The leading white colonists in the South Carolina low country were among the wealthiest people in the world.

The black population grew faster than the white population because plantations used numerous slaves to do all the work. In 1700, before the Yamassee War, the colonial population of South Carolina consisted of about 3,300 whites and 2,400 enslaved blacks. Ten years later, blacks outnumbered whites. By 1730, the total non–Native American population had grown to more than 30,000, and two out of every three people in South Carolina were slaves. In the low country near the coast, Africans soon outnumbered the white colonists nine to one. Groups of

By 1760, Charles Town had a population of about 8,000. The city was a center of colonial culture, with schools, libraries, and a theater.

slaves living in the low country developed their own language, **Gullah,** a mixture of several African languages that survives today on the islands and along the coast.

The King Takes Over

Most of the politicians in Carolina's government were wealthy plantation owners. Planters usually belonged to the Church of England, or Anglican church. However, people of other religions also settled in Carolina, drawn by the promise of religious freedom in the Carolina constitution. These included Baptists, Jews, Quakers, Presbyterians, and French **Protestants** (called Huguenots).

The Anglicans in control of the colony's government resented all the other religious groups and tried to limit

GULLAH: LANGUAGE THAT AROSE AMONG WEST AFRICANS LIVING ON THE COASTAL ISLANDS OF SOUTH CAROLINA AND GEORGIA; A MIXTURE OF COLONIAL ENGLISH AND SEVERAL AFRICAN LANGUAGES

their influence. They called the non-Anglicans "**Dissenters**" and passed laws barring them from government. In 1702, the Anglicans succeeded in declaring the Anglican church the established church of Carolina.

Carolina was governed as one large colony until 1712. The governor of Carolina directed the colony from Charles Town. A deputy governor supervised the Albemarle province, the name given to part of present-day North Carolina. The proprietors realized that the territory was too large to be governed effectively from a single capital at Charles Town. In 1712, the vast Carolina territory was divided and North Carolina and South Carolina officially became two separate colonies, each with its own government.

Over time, South Carolinians grew disgusted with the proprietors. The religious dissenters blamed the proprietors for letting the Anglicans take over the government. Dissenters and Anglicans alike blamed the proprietors for failing to help them when the Yamassee threatened the colony. The assembly rebelled against the proprietors, electing their own governor, the former

During the early 1700s, this building served as a country church for Anglican planters near Charles Town.

DISSENTER: MEMBER OF NON-ANGLICAN CHURCH WHO DISAGREED WITH ANGLICANS IN THE COLONIAL GOVERNMENT

King George I of Great Britain took over both Carolinas as royal colonies in 1729.

BRITISH: NATIONALITY OF A PERSON BORN IN GREAT BRITAIN; PEOPLE BORN IN ENGLAND ARE CALLED "ENGLISH"

militia officer James Moore Jr., in 1719. They wrote to the **British** king to ask for royal protection. In 1720, King George I sent a royal governor, Francis Nicholson, and arranged to buy the land of both North and South Carolina from the proprietors.

Religious Differences

Most of the wealthy people with political power in South Carolina belonged to the Anglican church. Most "up country" people belonged to other churches, such as Baptist or Presbyterian. The minister Charles Woodmason was a wealthy Charles Town Anglican. He considered it his sacred duty to endure any hardship in the effort to spread his religion to the inhabitants of the western counties. Woodmason traveled hundreds of miles to preach to frontier congregations throughout the western Carolinas during the late 1760s. He kept a diary of his travels.

Woodmason echoed the beliefs of other South Carolina Anglicans when he argued that religious freedom was bad for the people of Carolina. "Among the various plans of religion," he wrote, "they are at loss which to adopt, and consequently are without any religion at all . ... Among this medley of religions, true genuine Christianity is not to be found."

Unfortunately, other Charles Town Anglicans probably shared Woodmason's view of the up country and its people: "A finer body of land is nowhere to be seen—but it is occupied by a set of the most lowest vilest crew breathing—Scotch Irish Presbyterians from the north of Ireland. ..." He complained that there was "no bringing this tribe into any order. They are the lowest pack of wretches my eyes ever saw, or that I have met with in these woods— as wild as the very deer—no making them sit still during service. ... Such a pack I have never met with ... neither of one church or other ... not having ever seen a minister. ..."

There was one way, however, in which up country and low country people, rich or poor, Anglican or Presbyterian, did not differ. According to Woodmason, South Carolinians misspent the Sabbath day on "hunting, fishing, fowling, and racing ... frolicking ... drinking bouts and card playing ... Even in and about Charles Town, the taverns have more visitants than churches."

Several Anglican missionaries tried to convert slaves to Christianity and teach them to read the Bible. Most slave owners did not approve, because they found it more difficult to justify enslaving Christians. When Christian slaves attended church, they sat upstairs in a "slave gallery," built to keep them separate from the white congregation.

The eight original proprietors of North and South Carolina had died and most of their descendants were not making enough money from the colonies to remain interested in ownership. By 1729, all but one of the heirs agreed to sell their colonial land back to the king, and both North and South Carolina became royal colonies. The two Carolinas conducted a survey to set a dividing line between the colonies in 1737, but arguments continued to break out over where the line should be.

The South Carolina government was headed by a royal governor appointed by the king of **Great Britain**. The royal governor appointed the council, choosing from among the wealthy planters. The assembly was elected by free landowners. Both assemblymen and voters were required to own land, so the richest planters controlled the assembly. Local government was organized according to church parishes. Local officials such as sheriffs or justices were also appointed by the colonial government, and were chosen from among the wealthy and powerful.

Even among wealthy colonists, actual money was in short supply. Britain prohibited the colonies from making their own coins, so people used whatever scarce European or British coins happened to be circulating. More commonly, they simply bartered, or traded one kind of merchandise for another. Some used "bills of exchange," pieces of paper that were promises to pay a certain amount. Occasionally, colonial legislatures voted to print a limited amount of paper money, good only in that colony. South Carolina issued this currency in 1723.

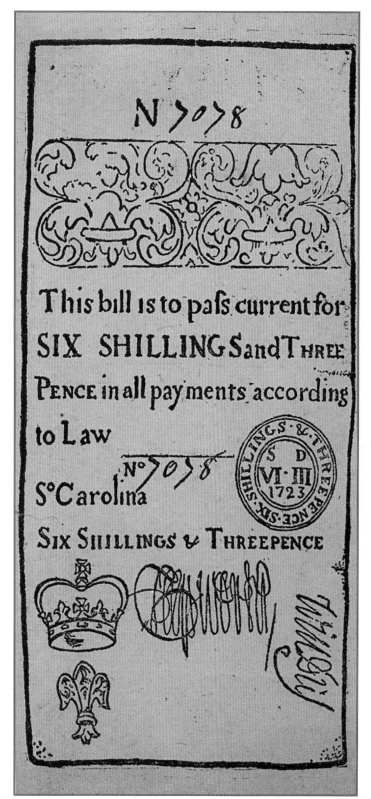

The Business of Slavery

South Carolinians had a never-ending demand for slaves. Due to overwork and disease, more slaves died than were born in South Carolina. Planters bought more male slaves than females, as they expected that men would be stronger and do more work in the fields. Planters eventually learned that slaves born in the colony had greater immunity to diseases and lived longer. Therefore, they began to import more women and encourage them to have children. Any children born to female slaves became the master's property.

South Carolina imported more slaves from Africa than did any other colony. Between 1700 and 1740, about 33,000 slaves from Africa arrived at Charles Town. In 1772, South Carolina imported about 5,200 slaves from Africa and 2,000 from the West Indies. Of these, 460 were sold to people in other colonies. Among the other colonies, only Virginia came close, importing about 2,000 slaves from Africa and the West Indies.

In the North American colonies, one could buy a slave for an average price of about 16 pounds (English money) in 1638. By 1775, the price had gone up to 44 pounds. The price varied by age, sex, and apparent strength and health of the individual slave. The purchase price of a slave in America was about two to five times higher than the price the trader paid in Africa.

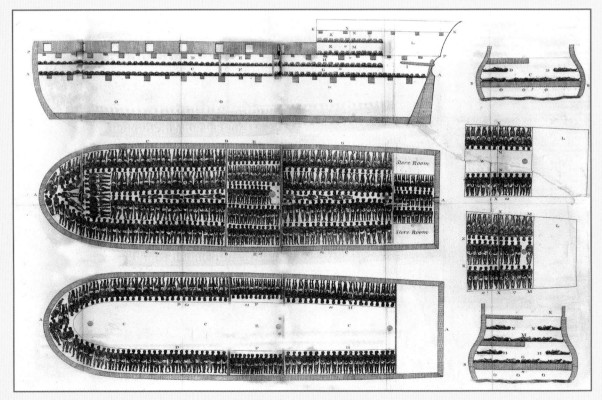

Each slave ship carried hundreds of chained and naked African captives. Many died on the voyage of starvation, cold, or disease, and their bodies were thrown overboard.

The town house of a wealthy merchant and planter, still standing in modern Charleston.

THE LOW COUNTRY

Planters and wealthy townspeople in the eastern part of the colony considered themselves to be of a higher social class than the more modest farmers and tradesmen. Many planters also owned fine houses in Charles Town and often visited the town with their families to join in the social life and political activities. In the summer they stayed in Charles Town to avoid the mosquitos and heat on their riverside plantations, leaving overseers in charge

Mulberry House, a fine South Carolina plantation house with its rows of slave cabins. Slave quarters were usually built of wood rather than brick, which was more expensive.

of the slaves. Many planters and their sons were also lawyers and politicians.

Slaves did all the hard work of growing and harvesting plantation crops. House slaves catered to their owners' every need, cooking and serving meals, cleaning, and even helping people bathe and dress. Most slave owners saw nothing wrong with owning people to do all their work. The wealthier they became, the more slaves they purchased, until slaves outnumbered free people in South Carolina. Slave labor, fertile soil, and a warm climate made South Carolina planters the richest in America. The planters displayed their wealth by buying fine clothing and furnishings, and by spending their ample free time hunting, horse racing, visiting, and throwing grand parties.

As the slave population surpassed the white population, fears of a slave rebellion grew. South Carolinians passed strict laws to control the slaves' every move. A settler in neighboring Georgia wrote that in South Carolina, "no Negro may go from one plantation to another unless he has

Planters enjoyed a pleasant social life. Peter Manigault, portrayed here with friends around 1750, was a member of one of South Carolina's leading families. The first Manigault arrived around 1695, worked as a tavern keeper, and branched out into other businesses such as barrel making. His son was the richest man in South Carolina, and his grandson, Peter, had a London education and became a lawyer active in the colonial government.

written permission from his master. The land is constantly patrolled, and also on Sundays one goes to church with swords, guns, and pistols, etc. The agitators of rebellion are punished in a very harsh and nearly inhuman way ... for example, slowly roasted at the fire." In fact, since 1724, South Carolina law had required planters to carry weapons to church, for fear that the slaves would rebel on a Sunday.

Slaves received inadequate food and little clothing. They lived in tiny cabins. There was nothing to stop cruel masters from whipping, torturing, or killing any slave that displeased them. When slaves married or had children, many owners made no effort to keep family members on the same plantation, selling children away from their mothers and wives away from their husbands.

In spite of the harsh controls placed on slaves in South

Carolina, a group of about 20 slaves staged a rebellion on a Sunday in September 1739. The slaves, many from the same part of Africa, communicated by beating drums and summoned their people. The rebels captured a store at Stono Bridge, near Charles Town, killing the owners and taking guns and ammunition. They were trying to march to Florida, where the Spanish, at war with Britain, offered freedom. As they marched along beating their drums to recruit others, more than 60 slaves joined them. The growing rebel force burned seven plantations and killed about 20 white people. The white colonists quickly assembled a militia, and within a day they captured and executed most of the rebels. South Carolina later passed a law to prohibit slaves from having drums.

Slaves loading the rice harvest on a cart

Plantation life was based on money made from **cash crop**s, crops that were produced in large amounts and sold. South Carolina planters grew mostly rice and indigo. These crops required a lot of labor to grow them successfully and prepare them for market. Indigo, a plant from which blue dye is made, was first grown successfully in South Carolina during the 1740s. Growing indigo and making the dye both required great care. Elizabeth Lucas, a teenage girl placed in charge of her family's plantation, grew the colony's first successful indigo crop from seeds her father sent from the West Indies. As a result of her experiments, by 1747, South Carolina was exporting 135,000 pounds of indigo dye. That number grew to over a million pounds a year before the Revolution.

UP COUNTRY

Beginning in the 1730s, South Carolina began to recruit new settlers. The people of the low country wanted to encourage more white people to settle in the colony as a counterweight to the growing black population. They also hoped that new settlers on the frontier would defend the eastern part of the colony against attacks by Native

CASH CROP: CROP—SUCH AS TOBACCO, RICE, OR COTTON—GROWN IN LARGE AMOUNTS TO BE SOLD FOR CASH

Indigo Pioneer

A young woman still in her teens was responsible for the success of indigo as a cash crop in South Carolina. Elizabeth Lucas was well educated and had a great deal of curiosity about farming. She also had the patience to try out new ideas when the old ones failed.

Elizabeth's father was a British army officer based in the West Indies. He moved his ailing wife and two daughters to one of his family's South Carolina plantations near Charles Town in 1738. The 600-acre riverside plantation was called Wappoo and had 20 slaves. Lucas then returned to the West Indies, leaving 15-year-old Elizabeth in charge, and sent her advice by letter. In 1740, Elizabeth wrote to a friend, "I have the business of 3 plantations to transact, which requires much writing ... by rising very early I find I can go through much business." She also took on the responsibility of tutoring her younger sister.

Lucas sent his daughter indigo seed from the island of Antigua. Elizabeth had some of the indigo planted each year, but the first few crops did poorly due to difficult weather conditions. In 1741, she wrote to her father: "We had a fine crop of indigo seed upon the ground ... and the frost took it before it was dry. I picked out the best of it and had it planted. ... I make no doubt indigo will prove a very valuable commodity in time ... . I am sorry we lost this season." She also had trouble with the dye-making process. The first good indigo crop grew on the Lucas plantation in 1744. Rather than make dye, Elizabeth saved the seeds and gave a lot of them to other planters so that they too could profit from growing indigo. She finally made money on indigo in 1745. Within two years, indigo was a major source of income to South Carolina planters.

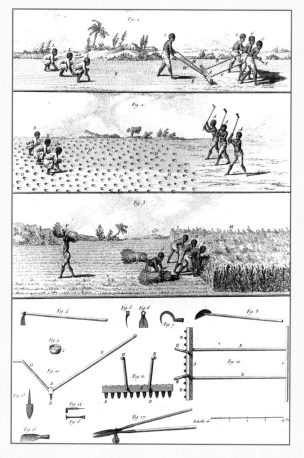

Slaves planted the indigo crop and harvested the plants once they flowered. The leaves and stems were then crushed in a vat. The indigo was left to ferment, and then beaten until flakes of blue dye formed. The dye then was allowed to settle to the bottom of the vat, and the liquid drained off. The flakes were pressed into cakes and sun-dried. The timing of the harvest, and the time that fermentation was stopped, were both critical to the quality of the dye's color. One mistake could ruin the whole year's production.

Much low -country transportation was by plantation-owned vessels along the rivers. Each riverside plantation had its own wharf for loading the harvest for the trip downriver to Charles Town.

Americans. The South Carolina government also helped the new settlement at Savannah, Georgia, in 1734, sending an official to organize the militia and negotiate with the Native Americans. South Carolinians were pleased to have the new colony as a buffer against attacks from the south.

The low country had filled up with plantations and the best land for growing rice was occupied, so new settlers and newly freed indentured servants received hilly land in the west. The higher lands were still suitable for growing indigo and other crops. Beginning in the 1750s, settlers from New York, Pennsylvania, and Virginia came to the South Carolina up country. Immigrants also sailed from Scotland, Wales, Ulster (Northern Ireland), Germany, and Switzerland to Charles Town, and from there moved up country.

As settlers moved west, their region was governed as an extension of the South Carolina low country. Local

Wheat did not grow well in the south, so Carolinians bought flour from Pennsylvania and New York. However, up country settlers grew corn, which they took to grist mills to be ground into cornmeal.

government officials were appointed in the low country rather than chosen from the local residents. These officials often stayed in the east and sent deputies to serve in their place. Western towns such as Camden and Ninety Six grew up around trading posts, grist mills, and courthouses.

Farmers who settled on South Carolina's western frontier lived as pioneers, clearing the trees off their land, building their own houses, and making their own furniture and clothing. Every member of the family, from an early age, shared the work of caring for crops and livestock. The majority did not own slaves. The fertile land rewarded their hard work with abundant crops and healthy animals.

Colonists carved their fields out of the forest by doing the exhausting work of cutting down trees and removing the stumps.

6.
A WORLD AT WAR

Colonists living on South Carolina's western frontier lived in fear of attacks by Native Americans.

Great Britain and Spain once again went to war in 1739. Known in America as King George's War, it lasted until 1748 and involved much of Europe and North America. James Oglethorpe of Georgia, commander of all militia forces on the southern frontier, visited Charles Town in 1740 to request help to attack the Spanish in Florida. South Carolinians were slow to respond. They had just put down a slave rebellion and their first concern was to defend their own colony from another such uprising. Nevertheless, about 400 South Carolinians joined Oglethorpe on his march to St. Augustine. Oglethorpe began a **siege** of the city but soon gave up and ordered a retreat. On their return to Charles Town, the South Carolina volunteers blamed Oglethorpe for his poor leadership.

When two years later, Oglethorpe again asked South Carolina for help in defending Georgia against a Spanish attack, the colonists were even less willing. Charles Town had recently suffered a huge accidental fire that destroyed much of the city. By the time South Carolina sent troops to Georgia, Oglethorpe had already repulsed the Spanish invasion.

THE FRENCH AND INDIAN WAR

The French traders of Louisiana and the British traders of South Carolina competed with one another for the friendship and loyalty of the Native Americans who lived between the two colonies. French traders sold firearms to the Native Americans but, unlike the British traders, did not encourage them to capture rival Native Americans as

After cutting down trees, the settlers squared up the logs to build log cabins. The Native Americans could see the changing landscape.

slaves. They wanted the Native Americans to stay loyal to the French and use the weapons to keep Carolinians away. However, the British had a better supply of trade goods than did the French, and their weapons were of higher quality, so many Native Americans preferred to trade with the British. On the other hand, the French traders treated the Native Americans with greater respect.

Above: Native American raids caused many frontier settlers to flee their farms.

As British colonists moved ever westward, settling on Native American hunting grounds, they did not pay much attention to the Native Americans' growing anger, or to the growing French military presence in the Ohio country beyond the mountains. The governor of Virginia sent the young militia officer George Washington to the Ohio country to warn the French that they were trespassing on British territory. Washington returned home with the alarming information that the French refused to leave.

The first battles between the English and the French took place in western Pennsylvania in 1754. They marked the beginning of a long world war whose battles raged on both sides of the Atlantic Ocean. France and Great Britain fought for control of territories in North America, the West Indies, Europe, and India. In America, the war came to be called the French and Indian War. In Europe the war was called the Seven Years' War.

Britain sent a large number of soldiers to North America to fight the French. In 1755, more than 1,000 troops landed in Virginia under the command of General Edward Braddock. Joined by George Washington and about 450 Virginia and Maryland soldiers, Braddock and his men marched straight across Virginia and into Pennsylvania, intending to capture a French fort.

General Braddock asked the other colonies to join him in marching on the Ohio country. South Carolina did not send aid, arguing that they needed all their money, resources, and men to defend their own frontier from the Native Americans. They also argued that they had to keep their militia in the east to guard against a possible slave uprising.

As the large army of red-coated British soldiers approached the Pennsylvania fort on a narrow wilderness path, they made an easy target for a surprise attack. On July 9, 1755, a small force of French and Native American men ambushed the army, shooting from the cover of the woods. In just three hours, they mortally wounded Braddock and killed more than 900 of his men, and lost only 43 of their own.

After Braddock's defeat, the surviving British soldiers marched off to fight in New York and Canada, leaving the southern colonists to defend their own frontiers as best they could. The disastrous defeat had left the western frontier open to numerous and deadly Native American

The Cherokees' friendship with the British was based on a treaty made in 1730 by seven Cherokee chiefs (below) on a visit to London. The treaty stated, "You ... have been deputed by the whole nation of the Cherokee Indians to come to Great Britain where you have seen the great King George and in token of your obedience have laid the Crown of your Nation with the scalps of your enemies and feathers of peace at his Majesty's feet." The treaty also promised that the king "has ordered his Governor to forbid the English from building houses or planting corn near any Indian town," and that "the Cherokees shall not suffer their people to trade with the white men of any other nation but the English nor permit white men of any other nation to build any forts, cabins or plant corn amongst them."

raids. The Native Americans burned settlers' cabins and killed their families. Hundreds of settlers abandoned their farms and fled to the east. In 1757 South Carolina asked Britain for help in defending their frontier against possible future French and Native American attacks. About 1,700 British troops came to South Carolina, but the assembly did not even vote for funding to provide the troops with food and supplies. The troops left in 1758.

The Cherokees, who controlled much of the Carolina frontier, at first remained loyal to the British. The up country settlers gradually turned the Cherokees from friends into enemies by moving onto Cherokee lands. Worse, some settlers killed and scalped Cherokees because Virginia offered a reward for Native American scalps.

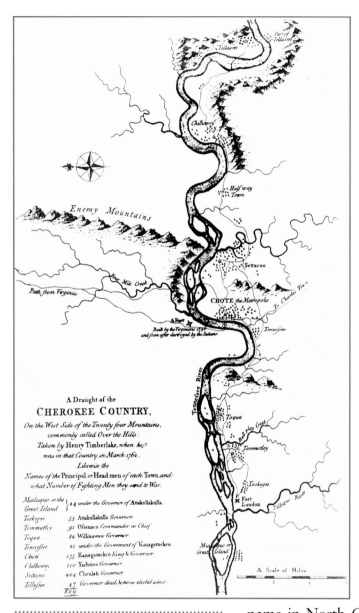

A Draught of the
CHEROKEE COUNTRY,
On the West Side of the Twenty four Mountains,
commonly called Over the Hills:
Taken by Henry Timberlake, when he
was in that Country, in March 1762.

Likewise the
Names of the Principal or Head men of each Town, and
what Number of Fighting Men they send to War.

Mialaquo, or the Great Island	24	under the Governor of Attakullakulla.
Toskegee	55	Attakullakulla Governor.
Tommotley	91	Ostenaco Commander in Chief
Toqua	84	Willinawaw Governor.
Tennefsee	21	under the Government of Kanagatucko.
Chote	175	Kanagatucko King & Governor.
Chilhowee	110	Yachtino Governor.
Settacoo	204	Cheulah Governor.
Tellafsee	47	Governor dead, & none elected since.
	809	

A Scale of Miles

After the Cherokees signed a new peace treaty with the British, their country along the Tennessee River, as shown by this 1762 map, was limited to the mountains of the western Carolinas and eastern Tennessee.

In 1759, Cherokees attacked and killed about 30 settlers. A party of 21 chiefs then arrived in Charles Town to try to negotiate for peace, but South Carolina militia took them hostage. When Native Americans attacked the fort where the chiefs were held, the soldiers executed the chiefs. In revenge, the Cherokees captured another fort and slaughtered the soldiers as they surrendered.

The Cherokees continued to attack frontier settlements. The British sent a force made up of Scottish Highlanders to invade Cherokee lands in 1761. They destroyed 15 Cherokee towns, along with all their food crops. The Cherokees, facing starvation, had no choice but to make peace. They were running out of ammunition, and they could no longer obtain it from the defeated French. The Cherokees and the English signed a treaty that gave the Cherokees the land west of a line along the crest of the western mountains.

Soon after the treaty was signed, white settlers flooded into the up country. Within a few years, three quarters of South Carolina's population lived in the western part of the colony. Unfortunately, the region also attracted outlaws. A so-called Regulator movement arose in the up country. Unlike the group of the same name in North Carolina, these Regulators asked for more government officials to enforce the law. They wanted local governments, courts, churches, and schools, along with the right to elect more representatives to the assembly. In sum, the **up-country** settlers wanted to be full citizens of South Carolina. In order to make their case more strongly, a band of armed Regulators marched to low country polling places and insisted on voting in elections. Government officials in Charles Town knew that they might need the up country people to help defend the colony at any time, so they tried to meet their demands.

7.
THE ROAD TO REVOLUTION

The British finally defeated the French at Quebec in 1759, and then won control of all of Canada. In 1763 France and Great Britain signed a peace treaty giving the British control of much of North America east of the Mississippi River. The costly war with France convinced the British government that the colonies should help pay for sending soldiers to America to defend colonists against Native Americans. Great Britain's **Parliament** imposed taxes on the colonists, and this enraged them. People throughout the colonies believed that a distant Parliament had no right to tax them and was violating their right to self-government.

The first major new tax law was the Sugar Act of 1764. The act called for import and export duties, or taxes, to be paid on many trade goods, such as sugar, coffee, indigo, and animal hides. Since the law did not tax rice, South Carolina's most important crop, the South Carolinians did not object to it.

> PARLIAMENT: THE LEGISLATURE OF GREAT BRITAIN

A 1775 view of the second oldest port in South Carolina, located on Port Royal Island. Merchants shipping goods through South Carolina's ports resentfully bore the burden of import and export duties imposed by the British government.

Next, in 1765 Parliament passed the Stamp Act. Under the Stamp Act, colonists had to pay to have most documents stamped, or risk arrest. Even newspapers had to have stamps. The Stamp Act affected colonists of all social classes. About 2,000 people demonstrated against the Stamp Act in Charles Town, and broke into the houses of stamp distributors. Groups calling themselves the Sons of Liberty formed in South Carolina and throughout the colonies to organize protests and to sabotage any efforts to enforce the Stamp Act. The South Carolina Sons of Liberty forced the colony's stamp agents to resign, and they prevented a ship from delivering stamps to the colony.

So unpopular was the Stamp Act that Parliament repealed it in March 1766. Still, King George III insisted that Great Britain's Parliament had the right to make laws for the colonies and collect taxes. Parliament passed a new set of laws taxing even more products, and angering more colonists. Tensions continued to grow between colonists and British soldiers and officials. Since the colonists did not have elected officials to represent them in Parliament, they objected to what they called taxation without representation. In South Carolina, British customs officers stirred up anger by seizing trading ships owned by prominent citizens.

The leaders of opposition to British laws formed Committees of Correspondence throughout the colonies. By writing letters, the Committees kept one another informed and made plans for the colonies to cooperate. They also planned to spread news that would influence public opinion in favor of rebellion. The Committees got all the colonies except New Hampshire to **boycott** English merchandise. The boycott convinced the British to repeal most taxes by 1770, except for the tax on tea.

Relieved of tax burdens for a while, the colonies prospered, and colonial life remained calm until 1773. Few colonists really wanted independence from England, as long as they could make their own laws and set their own taxes. Then Parliament passed a law that gave one British tea seller, the struggling East India Company, special treatment. The East India Company was given a

Henry Laurens was of French Huguenot ancestry and became rich as a merchant and rice planter. British customs officers seized his ships and earned his hatred. Laurens presided over South Carolina's first Provincial Congress, and went on to serve as president of the Continental Congress during the Revolution. He was on the committee assigned to negotiate a peace treaty at the war's end.

cheaply than any other dealer. Once again, the Committees of Correspondence went to work, spreading word of the new law and the coming East India Company tea shipments. The Sons of Liberty organized actions against the shipments.

The first such action, the famous Boston Tea Party, occurred in December 1773 with the dumping of a large tea shipment into Boston Harbor. South Carolinians tried to prevent a tea shipment from being unloaded in Charles Town, but they were outwitted by the customs officials, who quickly unloaded it and placed it in a warehouse. However, it remained there until **patriots** seized it during the Revolution.

When Britain responded to the Boston Tea Party by closing the port of Boston and placing Massachusetts under military rule, many in the colonies began to argue that they would have to fight for independence from Great Britain. They planned a meeting of the colonies in Philadelphia, to take place in September 1774. This meeting became known as the First Continental Congress. All colonies but Georgia agreed to participate.

The Congress drew up a set of resolutions stating the rights of the colonies to self-government and formed a Continental Association to boycott all trade with the British and organize local governments. South Carolina **delegates** insisted, however, that they still be permitted to sell rice to Britain, since much of the colony's economy depended on the sale of rice. By threatening to walk out, they made the other delegates give in. Finally, the delegates agreed to meet again in May 1775. Before they met again, the first battle of the American Revolution had been fought at Lexington and Concord in Massachusetts, in April 1775.

South Carolina formed a Provincial Congress to replace the royal government. As soon as news arrived of the fight in Massachusetts, the Provincial Congress moved to recruit and arm soldiers. It also formed a committee of safety to defend the colony from the British. The committee sent out ships to seize foreign ships carrying gunpowder. Patriots became suspicious of people who appeared to be loyal to Great Britain and had them arrested. In September 1775, the royal governor retreated to a British ship at anchor in Charles Town harbor.

Above: Another wealthy South Carolina merchant, Christopher Gadsden, also played a leading role in the colony's Revolutionary politics. He left the Continental Congress to serve as a general in the Continental Army, was captured by the British at Charles Town, and spent almost a year as a prisoner of war.

Below: Loyalists holding a secret meeting. Hundreds of loyalists moved back to Scotland or fled to Nova Scotia. The rebels confiscated their South Carolina properties.

The battle of Fort Moultrie prevented the British from capturing Charles Town in 1776. British cannonballs were unable to shatter the flexible palmetto wood of the fort's walls.

LOYALISTS: COLONISTS WHO WANTED AMERICA TO REMAIN A COLONY OF GREAT BRITAIN

to a British ship at anchor in Charles Town harbor.

At first many of the up country settlers remained loyal to Great Britain. Some were grateful for the British role in defeating the Cherokees. Others resented the wealthy and powerful planters of the low country who supported the Revolution. At least 150 armed clashes took place on South Carolina soil during the Revolution. Many of these fights were between **loyalist** and patriot colonists, with no British troops involved.

The first major fight came a few days before the signing of the Declaration of Independence. Four thousand South Carolinian troops assembled to defend Charles Town from an expected British attack. On June 28, 1776, British ships fired at an unfinished fort on Sullivan's Island in Charles Town harbor, but failed to capture it.

The British finally captured Charles Town in 1780. In another battle, a British commander allowed his men to slaughter Americans who were trying to surrender. This earned the hatred of many up country settlers,

The "Swamp Fox"

Francis Marion was an officer of the South Carolina militia during the Revolutionary War. He was equally effective in guerrilla actions or conventional battles. British officers nicknamed Marion "Swamp Fox" because he used his local knowledge well to strike at the enemy and then disappear into the swamps.

Francis Marion was born around 1732 to a French Huguenot family outside of Charles Town. He was an undersized, sickly child and never grew very tall as an adult. His family was not rich and Francis received very little education. Marion had hoped to become a sailor, but it is believed that he gave the idea up after surviving a shipwreck at the age of 16. Instead, he worked on his family's farm, and eventually earned enough money to buy a plantation.

Marion joined the colonial militia and first attracted favorable attention in the 1761 campaign against the Cherokees. When the Revolution began, he sided with the rebels, served in the Provincial Congress, and rejoined the militia. Marion then fought in the successful defense of Charles Town in 1776. After Charles Town fell to the British in 1780, Marion escaped to the swamps and gathered his legendary band of guerrillas. Their raids helped prevent British troops from taking control of the South Carolina countryside. Marion had the leadership ability to mold his irregular group of fighters into a bold and disciplined fighting force. He rose to the rank of brigadier general in the South Carolina militia, but he was only considered a colonel in the Continental Army.

After the Revolution, Marion served as a state senator and as commander of a fort. His plantation was wrecked by the British, and he needed to earn money to rebuild it. At the age of 54, he married and adopted a son. He died in 1795 at the age of 63. Francis Marion's courage and military accomplishments made him a legend. After the Revolution, people named their children, towns, and counties after him.

One story from the Francis Marion legend describes him offering sweet potatoes, the only food he had, to a captured British officer.

who then began fighting the loyalists and the British. Led by men such as Francis Marion and Thomas Sumter, the rebel **partisans** conducted a **guerrilla** war of brutal raids. Between raids they melted away into the countryside.

The tide turned against the British occupation of South

PARTISAN: FIGHTER WHO IS NOT PART OF A REGULAR ARMY OR MILITIA

GUERRILLA: SPANISH FOR "LITTLE WAR"; REFERS TO A TYPE OF WARFARE INVOLVING SURPRISE ATTACKS BY SMALL GROUPS OF FIGHTERS. GUERRILLA FIGHTERS ARE CALLED GUERRILLAS.

Carolina when a rough force of rebel backwoodsmen defeated British-led loyalist troops at Kings Mountain in October 1780. A few months later, in January 1781, American troops inflicted another major defeat on the British at Cowpens. Battle by battle, the Americans pushed the British back to Charles Town in 1781.

The so-called "over-mountain men" gather to march on the loyalists at King's Mountain.

EPILOGUE

After America won its independence from Britain in 1783, Charles Town was renamed Charleston. South Carolina became the eighth state to approve the United States Constitution on May 23, 1788. South Carolina delegates to the Constitutional Convention played a major role in keeping slavery legal in the new nation. Charleston remained the state capital until 1790, when the capital was moved to the planned town of Columbia in the center of the state.

Much of South Carolina's thickly wooded land was cleared of trees to make way for crops. Forests have since been allowed to grow back in many areas. However, the once-prevalent oak and hickory are less common. About two-thirds of the state's land area is wooded and lumber is an important industry in the state. The forests provide both softwoods for paper and hardwoods for furniture. The highland forests are still home to deer, bear, and wildcats.

After the Revolution, other nations began to compete with South Carolina in growing rice and indigo. Many planters turned to growing cotton, which became the state's most important crop. Cotton plantations depended on slave labor as well.

More than four million people live in modern South Carolina. Blacks, who had outnumbered whites from about 1720 until the early 20th century, today make up about 30% of the population. About 8,000 Native Americans, most of them Catawbas, live in the state, on a reservation near Rock Hill in the far north. A group of blacks of West African descent lived on the sea islands, isolated from the rest of South Carolina. They developed their own culture and language, called Gullah, a mix of African and old English. The island of Hilton Head, now a resort community with a mostly white population, was once a home to the Gullahs. About 25,000 Gullah people still live along the coast.

Half of the population lives in cities and towns. Columbia is the capital and largest city, and Charleston the second largest. About a third of the people work in manufacturing of chemicals, textiles, machinery, paper products, and plastic goods. Less than two percent work in agriculture, raising tobacco, soybeans, corn, cotton, peaches, poultry, and livestock. Fishermen bring in shrimp and other shellfish. On the coast, Parris Island is the site of a major U.S. Marine Corps base. Beach resorts line the coast and attract numerous visitors.

Colonial buildings still stand in the heart of Charleston. Nearby Charles Town Landing is a reconstructed village at the site of the colony's first settlement. The Charleston Museum, founded in 1773 and considered the nation's oldest museum, offers exhibits on the city's history.

Visitors to South Carolina can see Drayton Hall, Middleton Place and Boone Hall, plantations built near Charleston during colonial times. The old port town of Beaufort also has colonial houses still standing. The sites of several of South Carolina's Revolutionary War battles, including Fort Moultrie, Ninety Six, Camden, Kings Mountain, and Cowpens, are preserved in local and national parks.

A member of the colonial government built Drayton Hall around 1738. The house has been changed very little since it was built.

DATELINE

1521: A Spanish sea captain captures Native Americans on the coast of South Carolina and brings them to the West Indies as slaves.

1526: About 500 Spanish men and women, led by Lucas Vásquez de Ayllón, settle on the South Carolina coast, but abandon the settlement after many die of malaria or hunger.

1540: Hernando de Soto's expedition passes through the mountains of South Carolina.

1562: French Huguenots settle near present-day Port Royal, South Carolina, under the leadership of Jean Ribault, but abandon the settlement because of starvation.

1584: The first Englishmen, part of an expedition sponsored by Walter Raleigh, set foot on the coast of the present-day Carolinas. It is included in a vast area that Raleigh calls Virginia.

1629: King Charles I grants a huge territory, called Carolana, to Sir Robert Heath.

MARCH 24, 1663: King Charles II grants a charter to eight of his loyal supporters, renaming the territory Carolina.

APRIL 1670: Charles Town is established on the coast of present-day South Carolina.

1702: Governor James Moore sends an expedition to capture the Spanish town of St. Augustine, but the attack fails. The Spanish then march on Charles Town, but their attack also fails.

1712: Carolina is divided into two separate colonies, North Carolina and South Carolina.

1715–1716: The Yamassee War. Yamassee Indians, aided by the Creeks and Catawbas, attack English plantations in South Carolina.

1718: William Rhett captures the pirate Stede Bonnet. Bonnet and his men are executed at Charles Town.

1729: South Carolina becomes a royal colony.

1759: War breaks out between Cherokees and settlers on the South Carolina frontier. The two sides sign a peace treaty in 1761.

SEPTEMBER 1775: The royal governor flees Charles Town.

MAY 1780: The British capture Charles Town.

OCTOBER 1780: A force of rebel backwoodsmen defeats British-led loyalist troops at Kings Mountain.

MAY 23, 1788: South Carolina becomes the eighth state to approve the United States Constitution.

Glossary

ANGLICAN: belonging to the Church of England, a Protestant church and the state church of England

BOYCOTT: agreement to refuse to buy from or sell to certain businesses or people

BRITISH: nationality of a person born in Great Britain; people born in England are called "English."

CASH CROP: crop—such as tobacco, rice, or cotton—grown in large amounts to be sold for cash

CATHOLIC: Roman Catholic; the oldest Christian church organization, governed by a hierarchy based in Rome

CHARTER: document containing the rules for running an organization

DELEGATE: person elected to represent the voters' interests

DISSENTER: member of non-Anglican church who disagreed with Anglicans in the colonial government

DOMESTIC: tame, referring to animals such as livestock

FEUDAL: system in medieval Europe under which landless farmers lived and worked on land owned by others

FREEMEN: white, taxpaying males of at least 21 years of age who possess all the rights of citizenship, such as the right to vote, hold public office, or own land

FRONTIER: newest place of settlement, located the farthest away from the center of population

GREAT BRITAIN: nation formed by England, Wales, Scotland, and Northern Ireland; the term "Great Britain" came into use when England and Scotland formally unified in 1707.

GUERRILLA: Spanish for "little war"; refers to a type of warfare involving surprise attacks by small groups of fighters. Guerrilla fighters are called guerrillas.

GULLAH: language that arose among West Africans living on the coastal islands of South Carolina and Georgia; a mixture of colonial English and several African languages

HUGUENOTS: French Protestants

INDENTURED SERVANT: person who has agreed to work as a servant for a certain number of years in exchange for food, clothing, a place to sleep, and payment of one's passage across the Atlantic to the colonies

LOYALISTS: colonists who wanted America to remain a colony of Great Britain

MALARIA: potentially fatal disease spread by mosquitos

MERCHANT: trader; person who buys and resells merchandise

MILITIA: group of citizens not normally part of the army who join together to defend their land in an emergency

NOBILITY: members of the high British social class just below royalty, possessing titles or ranks that were either inherited or given by the king or queen

PARLIAMENT: the legislature of Great Britain

PARTISAN: fighter who is not part of a regular army or militia

PATRIOT: American who wanted the colonies to be independent of Great Britain

PIEDMONT: hilly region between the low country and the mountains

PLANTATION: large estate where a cash crop is grown, usually farmed by slaves

PLANTER: owner of a large estate, called a plantation

PROPRIETOR: private owner

PROTESTANT: member of any Christian church that has broken away from Roman Catholic or Eastern Orthodox control

SIEGE: campaign to capture a place by surrounding it, cutting it off from supplies, and attacking it

SUBSISTENCE: producing just enough food or income to survive

UP-COUNTRY: Piedmont and mountain regions of South Carolina

WEST INDIES: islands of the Caribbean Sea, so called because the first European visitors thought they were near India

FURTHER READING

Branch, Muriel Miller. *The Water Brought Us: The Story of the Gullah-speaking People.* New York: Cobblehill Books, 1995.

Long, Cathryn J. *The Cherokee.* San Diego: Lucent Books, 2000.

Smith, Carter, ed. *Battles in a New Land: A Source Book on Colonial America.* Brookfield, Conn.: Millbrook Press, 1991.

Smith, Carter, ed. *Daily Life: A Source Book on Colonial America.* Brookfield, Conn.: Millbrook Press, 1991.

Smith, Carter, ed. *Explorers and Settlers: A Source Book on Colonial America*. Brookfield, Conn.: Millbrook Press, 1991.

Smith, Carter, ed. *The Revolutionary War: A Source Book on Colonial America*. Brookfield, Conn.: Millbrook Press, 1991.

WEBSITES

http://www.americaslibrary.gov
Select "Jump back in time" for links to history activities

http://cfmedia.scetv.org/schistory/
See a slide show of South Carolina history from pre-Colonial to modern times

http://www.thinkquest.org/library/JR_index.html
Explore links to numerous student-designed sites about American colonial history

BIBLIOGRAPHY

Gallay, Alan. *Voices of the Old South: Eyewitness Accounts, 1528–1861*. Athens, Ga: University of Georgia Press, 1994.

Lefler, Hugh, ed. John Lawson. *A New Voyage to Carolina*. Chapel Hill, N.C.: University of North Carolina Press, 1967.

Middleton, Richard. *Colonial America: A History, 1607–1760*. Cambridge, Mass.: Blackwell, 1992.

Salley, Alexander S., Jr. *Narratives of Early Carolina, 1650–1708*. New York: Charles Scribner's Sons, 1911.

Taylor, Alan. *American Colonies*. New York: Viking, 2001.

Heritage History of the Thirteen Colonies. New York: American Heritage Publishing Co., 1967.

Weir, Robert M. *Colonial South Carolina: A History*. Millwood, N.Y.: KTO Press, 1983.

Index

Africa 6, 22-23, 36
Ayllón, Lucas Vásquez de 8

Barbados; see West Indies
Barnwell, John 27
Berkeley, John 13
Berkeley, William 13
Bonnet, Stede 29
Boston Tea Party 53
Braddock, Edward 48

Canada 48, 51
Carteret, George 13
Charles I 12
Charles II 12, 16
Charles Town 16, 21-22, 24-26, 28-32, 37, 45, 50, 53-54, 57-59
climate 18, 24
Colleton, John 13
Columbus, Christopher 7
Continental Congress 53
Cooper, Anthony Ashley 13
Craven, William 13

De Soto, Hernando 8
Drake, Francis 10

France 7-9, 25, 46-51
French and Indian War 48-51
frontier 44-45, 48-50

geography 17
George I 33
Georgia 43, 45
government 12-13, 31-33, 35, 44, 50, 53
Gullah 31, 58

Heath, Robert 12
Hilton, William 14-15, 20
Hyde, Edward 13

Indians; see Native Americans
indigo 41-43, 51

King George's War 45
Kings Mountain 57, 59

Laurens, Henry 52
Lucas, Elizabeth 41-42

Manigault, Peter 40
Marion, Francis 55
Monck, George 13
Moore, James (governor) 25
Moore, James, Jr. 27

Native Americans 8, 18-22, 25-29, 46-50, 58
  Catawba 18, 27-28
  Cherokee 18, 27-28, 49-50
  Congaree 18
  Creek 26-28
  Cusabo 18, 21-22, 27
  mound builders 18
  Santee 18
  Savannah 22, 26-27
  Sewee 18
  Tuscarora 27-28
  Wateree 18
  Westo 18, 21-22, 27
  Yamassee 18, 26-28, 32
naval stores 24
Nicholson, Francis 33

North Carolina 27, 32, 35

Oglethorpe, James 45-46

Parris Island 10
pirates 29
plantations 15-16, 22, 24-25, 28-29, 37-39, 41-42
population 16, 18, 29-30, 58
Port Royal 9, 14, 16, 28, 51

Raleigh, Walter 10
religion 9, 12, 15, 31-32, 34
Revolutionary War 53-57
Rhett, William 29
Ribault, Jean 9
rice 24, 41, 43, 51, 53

St. Augustine 10, 25-26, 45
slaves 6, 8, 15-16, 21-28, 30, 36, 39-42, 46
social class 34-35, 37
Spain 7-10, 25-26, 45-46
Stamp Act 52
Sugar Act 51

trade 19, 21-24, 26-30, 46-47, 51

Verrazano, Giovanni da 9
Virginia 12-13, 21, 48

Washington, George 48
West Indies 8, 13-16, 21-22, 24, 36, 41-42, 48
White, John 19
Woodmason, Charles 34
Woodward, Henry 22
women 16, 22, 28, 36